Paula's book "Why am I So Happy" is one-of-a-kind just like Paula. This book is recommended for everyone of all ages whether you need a reminder on gratitude and the definitions of joy and happiness, you're going through some rough times, and/or if you're completely happy this book has great examples and techniques that you can use in your everyday life. It also makes as a great gift for a close one.

Carly Calabrese, Career Coach/Professional
Marketer/Writer/LinkedIn Consultant

I've been blessed to know Paula Neva Vail for over two years and in that time she has enriched my life enormously with her kindness, support and invaluable wisdom, which she is always excited to share. She has a consistent positive attitude for life and is brimming with love for everyone around her. Her healing energy is palpable and easily felt in her presence and when she sends the gift of Reiki from miles away. Paula's many projects in television; radio and print are filled with the purity of her heart, touching countless lives and making the world a brighter place. She is truly an inspirational beacon, mentor and embodiment of an earth-bound angel who I am lucky enough to call my friend.

Rob Leonetti, Empowerment &
Transformational Strategist

I was thinking this morning what to write that captures the true essence of Paula and her gifts. As I was contemplating my words, the song "The Power of Love", by Huey Lewis and the News, came on the radio, and I thought, "This is it! This is Paula!"

Paula is the power of love from her loving touch as a Reiki Master, to the gift of her kindness, to the aura of joy she spreads to all. I have always enjoyed reading her publications because you can feel this warmth in her words as well.

This lovely woman has faced her own adversities, challenges and sorrow, but through it all, she has always managed to find the positive, the lesson, and the gratitude in every situation. Her new book, "Why Am I So Happy" will motivate us all to find joy and happiness in every aspect of life!

Julie Sherwood, Certified Wellness Coach

"At FiveD.TV: The Next Dimension Network we thoroughly enjoying carrying TV Host Paul Vail's video interviews that encourage audiences to expand their mind, open their hearts and embody higher soulful qualities so as to better shape the communities they live in and hence raise the consciousness of the planet as a whole."

Lana Marconi, Producer, FiveD.TV

I met Paula at a time of deep grief and change in my life. Paula's loving positive energy and words shifted the place I was in with such ease and grace. My life has been so enriched from the very first moment we met. I had the privilege to travel to Africa with Paula this past year, and experience firsthand how she truly lives in joy and happiness. She finds joy in every day.

Her loving, happy energy was always present. The saying, "Your energy introduces you before you even speak" is so genuine with Paula. Every day I saw people light up just from the loving, genuine spirit she radiates.

Paula has experienced hardships, loss, and her own life challenges, which she has touched on in her book, yet she chooses to be "happy" regardless of the circumstances.

I have been inspired by her ability to find joy every day. She radiates the most loving energy, a compassionate heart and a depth of wisdom that is rare. Paula's teaching from her Reiki, to her Radio/TV talks shows, to everyday life provide a loving, healing blessing to this world. She brings happiness from the inside and shares it with the world.

I have no doubt this book "Why Am I So Happy" will touch lives, and hearts like Paula herself. She is truly dedicated to living a life of joy and love, and helping people live in this same energy, and find it within themselves.

Rhonda Buston, Retired Veteran,
U. S. Coast Guard, Reiki Practitioner

Paula has been a great mentor and true friend and my life has changed for the better because of her. She is a true inspiration who has an aura that radiates love, peace, kindness, wisdom and "happiness".

If you want to feel her positive energy, kindness, gratitude and the love she has then "Why Am I So Happy" is a read for you. "Why Am I So Happy" will put a smile on your face and help you define what joy and happiness really is.

Cheryl Fletcher, Office Administrator, Law Firm

WHY AM I SO HAPPY?

PAULA NEVA VAIL

AUTHORS PLACE
— PRESS —

Published by Authors Place Press
9885 Wyecliff Drive, Suite 200
Highlands Ranch, CO 80126
Authorsplace.com

Manufactured in the United States of America.

ISBN: 978-1-62865-621-3

CONTENTS

INTRODUCTION

"Really, Paula! Why are you so happy all the time?"

This question is a common one that has propelled me to write this book. All of my life, I have been asked by others, "Why are you so Happy?" Oftentimes, I was caught with a big smile on my face. Other times, I'd shared a kind word with someone. Frequently, I danced to a song that I heard playing somewhere nearby me, only to be caught in the act by onlookers. These spontaneous reactions occurred often without my thinking about why I was filled with joy.

Of course, this does not mean there weren't times in my life that I had to choose to smile and recognize the joy in my life. Like most, I have seen tragedy, heartbreak, and experienced sadness and challenges. Throughout my life's history, I have experienced mistreatment and disrespect, the loss of loved ones, and financial stress, as so many of us do. However, I believed early in my life that I was the one in charge of my emotions. Even though, at times, I yearned for happiness—often from other people and outside circumstances.

In this book, I will share with you what I personally believe are the tools to open the door to the incredible happiness that resides in each and every one of us—a joy that is in the center of our being. A joy that can be triggered or tapped into.

I have always felt great joy in seeing others happy. The completion of this book is my expression of love and caring for humans, as well as for the animal kingdom, and our beautiful planet. Did you realize that animals feel our happiness when we are happy? It's true!

Internal joy creates a beautiful energy within and around us. Everyone can make a difference in the world. Every day is a *new day*! Whatever your background, history, or circumstances are, you wake up to a new day, every day.

What exactly does that mean for us?

New choices. New attitude. Personal manifestation. Each day, we greet these opportunities. It's entirely up to us whether we seize them or we allow them to pass us by.

CHAPTER 1

"CHOICES"

"Attitude is a choice. Happiness is a choice. Giving is a choice. Optimism is a choice. Kindness is a choice. Whatever choice you make, makes you. Choose wisely."

~ Roy T. Bennet

What is happiness exactly?

Let's answer that question by looking at who we really are. Our true essence is joy—something found inside each and every one of us.

I suspect, a few of you doubt this. Why does it matter? How does doubt even develop? Well, it matters a great deal because your attitude is the core that creates your happiness. Fortunately, you control your attitude—no one else does.

Passion, fun, creativity, relationships, exercise—all of these things and more, constitute part of happiness. The challenges in life don't have to be deterrents to happiness. They can be a different path taken. In fact, making an observation that others don't experience challenges is a false observation—and not a factor in your personal happiness. The power of gratitude is a powerful tool which brings about happiness from within. Resistance from outside sources or from others can actually empower us. When we encounter resistance in our path or desired creation, we have two choices:

- Choice number One: allow the resistance to deter us or give us doubt. At times, we may even surrender our dreams of happiness. Often, resistance can come to us by others who, themselves are yearning for happiness, and actually believe they feel better in knowing others are not happy, as they are not. We can see resistance they throw at us as an example of the direction of their own thoughts. Which has nothing to do with our happiness, unless we allow it.

- Choice number Two: The challenge or resistance that we are facing can light the fire inside us to continue to move forward! As well as telling ourselves that our desire is possible, this can be an opportunity for us to react with compassion to outside negativity and resistance and that we have Source manifestation guiding us. Also, our own unique ability to direct our own thoughts and actions, reminds us once again that if we choose to be happy, no one can stop us!

Life is a precious gift not to be wasted. The connections we make, and the experiences we have in life, are not meant to resist joy. Consider this: to surrender is not a weakness—it is allowing. Don't chase life, allow it. The beauty inside of us is more than just a physical state, it is more than an emotion. Our physical body is where we reside throughout this lifetime. We can love and nourish our beautiful and amazing body, even as we acknowledge that it is temporary.

Feelings are that way too. The emotions that we choose to focus on can be beautiful, heartfelt, and a source of happiness for ourselves and others around us. These two beautiful traits are an extension of the unique essence of our inner being. Our inner core, our higher self, our soul planner, is forever an essence and beauty that continually takes us from lifetime to lifetime. When we choose the direction of our thoughts, we are giving a message to our higher self – a request, actually. Our higher self will give this energy to the beautiful manifestation river in which we flow in everyday life, thus attracting more of what we ask for. It is possible to ask and not even realize we are doing it.

Another confirmation is the importance and power of our thoughts. We can make the choice to be grateful, joyous, and aware—to be ever watchful of the guidance that we are given every day. Take a moment each day to clear your mind, thank your higher self, choose to be in alignment with your higher self, and open your heart and mind to the incredible guidance from your higher self. Make this a daily routine and just accept your beautiful creativity. The positive manifestation we can tap into is easily beyond our greatest desires or expectations. As we progress through life, we cannot change the past but we can change how we view our personal history. We can choose the perspectives from which we have gained from our experiences.

A new outlook can literally change the direction of our path going forward. When we awaken our heart's awareness to the power of love, we access the gifts of the universe. When our actions and activities become gratifying and purposeful in serving self and others, we do not tire because we are doing what we are meant to do.

A personality that is engaged in the work of its higher self is not burdened with negativity—it does not doubt or fear. Instead, this personality delights in its work.

When we suffer pain and experiences that are disappointing, we can also realize that these experiences are doorways to a new awareness. As you work with trust and strength, fear slowly disintegrates. When fear ceases to be frightening, it cannot remain.

When we choose to evolve consciously, we give permission to be shown the fullest of our power and to be guided in using that power. If we do not trust, we limit what the universe can do to help us. This is because we stand in the way of the blessings that are waiting for us.

The final step in reaching authentic, life-enhancing abundance and change, is to say, "Yes!" Know that so much joy, love, and manifestation is meant for you.

You need only to allow.

When we are happy, our body vibrates at a higher frequency than when we are sad. This brings blessings and the ability to manifest. Recognize yourself as a being of frequencies. Frequency is in everything. Anything that happens has a frequency. We can transform our personality to a higher frequency, if desired. This does not come without effort—it takes work to realign our personal habits. Such habits include: attitude, behaviors and emotions.

When we become aware of our habitual responses and put in motion the power of our positive intentions, we can release the lower vibrational energies that affect our lives. When we choose joy and gratitude, we transform our vibrational frequencies to a higher enlightened level. Then, we affect our manifestation, health, and emotions. Our entire energy field will be affected and will create change.

When we let our personality engage in low vibrational emotions, like jealousy, hatred, non-forgiveness, judgment, and brutality, we are feeding our soul vibrational arsenic. These behaviors destroy the strength of our soul (or higher self). On the other hand, love, compassion, trust, and forgiveness enable our higher self to flourish and shine.

If you are aware of guidance from your higher self, and you are receptive to it, you raise your vibrational energy. This allows guidance of flow instantly and continually into your life.

When we experience fear, anger, or jealousy, we are in an illusion. These things do not actually exist. They are emotions and beliefs we allow into our mindset. That is why pursuing them does not bring power! Existing at the level of our higher self is…love.

Understand that this is the power of awareness!

CHAPTER 2

"EMOTION TRIGGERS"

Some believe our thoughts come in random spurts—that we are unable to control what "pops" into our brains. Nothing could be further from the truth!

In actuality, we consciously choose the direction of our thoughts even though we may not always realize it. These choices activate a phenomenon I call "emotion triggers."

The following are some examples of what I mean:

- Seeds of doubt and fear may be planted by a focus on what we have not yet achieved. This causes a cycle of emotion that leads to depression and sadness. However, if we look at what we do not have as an opportunity to manifest our goals, we instead trigger excitement and creativity, which then also triggers joy.

- Emotions such as blame, anger, and resentment can be triggered when we continually focus on mistreatment or tragedy. Doing so causes sadness, depression, and lack of inspiration. In a different light, we can choose to see today as a "new day"—an opportunity to release attachments to past events, and step into freedom and empowerment. This, then, triggers happiness and a passion for the future we are creating.

- What if our focus is to take a stand against the cruelty and tragedy in the world? We can become elevated and motivated by knowing that one person can truly make a difference in the lives of those touched by our actions. As we focus on the possibilities that we can achieve, we become triggered, once again, to be happy, excited, and motivated.

- A focus on gratitude automatically brings thoughts that search for aspects in our lives that we appreciate and enjoy. This will create a loving, happy feeling within.

These examples range from people we care about, friends, relatives, co-workers, pets, possessions, weather, scenery, wildlife, beauty, art, music, projects, accomplishments, health, food, abilities…the list is endless.

Take a moment now to ask yourself this question: What percentage of my day is focused on the *positives* in my life, as compared to the *negatives* in life?

So, how then do we choose joy?

We live in the moment. Only in the moment.

While being present is paramount to joy, it is also important to give acknowledgement to our past. This is the place of memories, of our fulfilment, and/or regrets.

Now is when we feel the love of Source in our entire being. ***Now*** is when we feel self-love and love for others. ***Now*** is when we honor our physical body. ***Now*** is when we are awakened.

Think about living souls outside of yourself and other human beings —the animal kingdom and other life on the planet. ***Now*** is when we all feel loved and cared for by others. Listening to the ***now*** is when we feel the energetic connection with ourselves to Source and these other life entities. When we realize that we are energetically connected to others, we create more compassion in our hearts. Compassion creates increased self-love and joy that manifests into helping and caring about others.

So, then, do others control our happiness? Only if we allow it. As we progress through this lifetime, we may find ourselves focused on pleasing others to gain happiness. Happiness already belongs to us. It comes from deep within. Searching for happiness through the approval of others is actually a false assumption. The very people to whom we hand over that power may turn on us—by disapproving of our actions the next day, the next month, or the next year.

How can the joy and happiness that is within our loving soul remain under a false premise, such as this? It cannot, because this requirement for happiness is conditional. Remember, love, joy and happiness is constant. Our exterior personality and our intention are key to determining where we reside on the "happiness scale."

Fortunately, we can find great satisfaction in accomplishments and the gratitude of those around us. A feeling of appreciation toward others and received from others is a beautiful, joyous gift, indeed. Celebrate that gift.

When we realize that it is impossible to please everyone, we discover that pleasing ones self is what counts. Searching for happiness through the approval of others is actually a false joy. When another makes the decision for happiness on our behalf, how can the joy and happiness that is within our loving soul come to life? It can't. Because, under those circumstances, our personal happiness is conditional. True happiness is *not* conditional. It is merely a choice, a choice we make every day.

Loving and appreciating ourselves as the beautiful individuals we are allows us to become a shining light and inspiration to others. Carry that joy and inspiration with you every day. Witness what that beautiful energy can manifest.

Many of us are told that if we want to manifest our dreams and goals, we simply make a list, voice an affirmation, and wait for the desired outcome. Unfortunately, there is one very important key missing in this how-to-manifest list.

TRUST!

If we envision our success and say our affirmations without trust, to a degree, the words are empty. Barriers of doubt, fear and worry may follow our intention. These barriers can be a wall to block us from success. Ultimate manifestation connects us to the beautiful flow of Source and the creative abundance and guidance waiting for us. Source, the angels, and the positive energy we have access to will be with us—we only need to ask. Trust allows us to "jump feet first" into the beautiful loving river of manifestation. It's wonderful to have goals and dreams, but if we focus on only those goals, we actually block other manifestations from being able to occur.

One of the most important recommendations I wish to share with you is to keep the door open to other unconsidered possibilities. *Trust in Source to connect you to manifestations beyond your goals. Source can connect us to that which is beyond our wildest dreams.* It's so true!

I see it like this. Our goals, desires, and accomplishments lay in one hand, while trust and peace lay in the other. We are always communicating to Source what we most desire—those things that we wish to pull into our lives. Great strength comes through our thoughts.

Let's just put on the brakes for a moment and look at how powerful that is. Our thoughts not only direct what we do and perceive in the moment, they also direct our future path and manifestation.

Our thoughts and words have tremendous power!

The good news is that we can learn how to direct that power to create amazing possibilities in life. We, alone, make that choice. Our beliefs "that which we have faith in", will come back to us through what we attract.

For example, my Reiki practice is an area in which some say I should be cautious. I've been advised that I should worry about receiving negative energy from others when I offer the beautiful loving gift of Reiki to others. Actually, in any situation, you may encounter someone else's negative energy.

I believe that when we have trust in the love and light that we are surrounded in, we are protected in our path. We need not carry fear and worry because we choose to resonate in a positive energy. We couldn't be more protected. This is first and foremost. Love is the greatest power!

With our thoughts and words, we create what we ask for. This is a truth I have experienced first-hand. To explain this point further, consider this example: If we say, "I want to write a fantastic book, but I'm not sure I can. I may not be able to publish it," etc. (you get the self-doubt picture in this scenario), we give the energy to (and ask for) those barriers to occur.

However, the opposite can be achieved. If we say something to the effect of, "I am creating a book which will be a positive guide to others," or, "I see the success of my writings that I will share with the world," we open the door to making those aspirations become reality. With just a change in perspective, we can actually visualize the event as already accomplished. In doing so, with this perspective, we give that energy to Source manifestation.

We are able to choose and focus on what we want as an outcome – a very powerful alternative to a focus on what we don't want. Create the habit of putting forth *positive thoughts and words*. When you do, you will see manifestations unfold beyond your greatest desires.

Create your own positive words and vision. Make them unique to your life's path.

> "There are only two ways to live your life. One is as though nothing is a miracle. The other is as though everything is a miracle"
>
> **~Albert Einstein**

So, what are you waiting for?

CHAPTER 3

"ILLUSIONS"

When we give into the illusion of low vibration energies, it takes power over us. When we rise above low vibration energies, we have authentic self-empowerment. False illusions have no power over you when you love and allow compassion and wisdom to open your heart, and raise you to a higher vibration frequency. At this time, creativity and joy will flow into the present moment. This will also draw other souls with the same frequency of consciousness closer to you. Which can be truly amazing.

When we live in a high vibration frequency, we allow new opportunities, relationships, and guidance into our lives. Fear, anger, and jealousy are very low vibration energies. These emotions put us at a very low frequency level. If anger or fear builds within the personality, the world it lives in reflects the anger and the fear until, ultimately, the personality will create its own experience and perception at this level.

Just as the frequency of anger evokes some "like frequency" in the consciousness, the frequency of love awakens also "like" responses.

It is the intention that determines the effect. This is a powerful message and great wisdom, in my opinion.

The human emotional system has two elements: fear and love. Love is of the higher self, while fear is of the personality.

The emotions we choose lead to our corresponding behaviors. Our emotions will spill out of our personal energy sphere and into the collective energy of those around us, creating either negative or positive karma. This also, is a powerful message.

When our thoughts and intentions include trust and love (not fear and ego), everything changes in our life's path. When we choose to look at the situation with love, compassion, and other high frequency energies, this aligns the situation to a higher frequency level. As well as aligning us with positive frequency manifestations that come to us. This guides us to becoming a presence not a person. We are then truly connected to totality.

The final step in reaching authentic power is releasing to a higher level of wisdom and creativity. Striving to live each day in a higher vibration frequency, through our thoughts and emotions, will bring balance and new manifestations.

Sometimes, however, it is difficult to see the positive in every situation.

To understand this from my perspective, let me share some personal history about myself.

I was born a premature baby. I was not expected to survive the night. Yet, I did survive. This has caused me to take my life seriously and blessed me with a heart of gratitude and appreciation for all that I have been given—especially the gift of life itself.

I began working in an Italian restaurant during my college years. This began as a base employee position, progressed to manager, then finally, the owner of my own restaurant—all taking place within a span of 27 years. I loved my customers and the work of customer service. I also love the family blessings I was given – three children, specifically.

My family was, and still is, a priority in my life.

While my children were young, I chose to spend time with them. Those were precious years. To facilitate that goal, I opened a daycare in my home and watched over children for eight years. During the weekdays I would work doing daycare and at nights and weekends, I would work at the restaurant. For months, I would work with no days off. As I look back, those were some of the best years of my life! Cherished memories. I had so much fun during that time.

But then life changed. My husband became ill and, after several surgeries, he also became addicted to the pain medicine prescribed to him. I watched as he became a completely different person. He went from loving life to questioning it. He became angry and depressed. Also, adding excessive alcohol consumption to the drugs he was taking. Our happy home was torn apart. As I watched this unfold, I felt so helpless and lost. I had to make the decision to find a new home for the children and myself. I stayed in contact with him, and later discovered that he had become homeless. I then secured an apartment for him and got him off the streets.

His addiction continued and his health declined. Sadly, he eventually passed away as a result. To this day, when I see a homeless person on the street, I ask myself "What are their circumstances? Why are they in this setting? I will not judge them because I don't know what obstacles they have encountered. There is great controversy about giving money to the homeless. I feel that when you offer to help someone with food, cash etc. it is an act of kindness. How they proceed with what they have received is their personal choice. Having compassion and kindness is a choice we make every day. As time went by, I continued to run the restaurant and take care of my family, which was a great passion for me, as well as a responsibility that I took seriously. Some days, I would bring my kids with me to work, creating a family bond in the fun of working in a restaurant setting – part of my decision to choose happiness. I survived by pushing myself to choosing happiness and gratitude *every single day*.

Then the time came for me to make changes in my life. I remarried and sold my restaurant. Subsequently, I needed a new job and chose to work as a receptionist because I wanted to continue working with the public. About that time is when I discovered the beautiful modality of "Reiki." I started training in Reiki energy healing to help my beloved dog, who was suffering with her own illness. Immediately, I saw the benefits that Reiki healing provided her. I knew this was something I had been guided to do and decided to take my training to higher levels. This decision turned into a new career.

Soon afterward, I was approached by an online radio network to do a show about Reiki. It wasn't long until the show became tremendously successful. I discovered a joy and passion that I had not envisioned. Through this show, I was able to share many amazing guests with my listeners. I continue to do radio and tv shows, teach Reiki classes, and offer personal mentoring to Reiki practitioners to this day. Mostly, I do this because I want to be a positive energy in the world.

One of my daily affirmations include: "I say yes to helping others, animals and the world." We choose everyday what we would like our influence in the world to be.

Take a moment to realize and create the vision you have for your legacy in the world. What energy are you sharing with the world?

I believe that when we strive to be a positive energy in the world, positive energy comes back to us multiplied. I wake up every day grateful and excited for what each new day will manifest. My goal is to be an example and supporter of others, in that they can achieve magnificent manifestations and fire joy into their own lives.

CHAPTER 4

"IMPRESSIONS"

How do you talk to yourself?

How do you present yourself to others?

Remember the adage: "You never have a second chance to make a first good impression." There is truth in that statement. The first impression we make resides with others forever.

Our first impression is powerful.

How do we address that with confidence? Ask yourself, "Do I wish to present what I believe they wish me to be?" Or, "Do I wish to honor and value the beautiful person I am by presenting my true self to others?" When we give our true selves the love and respect we deserve, and gratitude for our unique and beautiful selves, we are giving ourselves permission to "be who we are" and to "show others who we really are."

When I was young and struggling with low self-esteem, and being bulled in school, I wanted to be "good enough" in the eyes of others. At that time, I was given some wise inspiration by my dear uncle Ernie. I decided then that my attitude would be, "Love me or don't." That decision set me free.

As human beings, I realize that we aren't perfect, we make mistakes, but that we all have our own gifts, talents, and passions that are unique to each of us. These traits are truly things to celebrate. I choose to be who I am and let others make their own judgements about me.

We can't control what others think of us, but we can control what we think of ourselves. So, why give others our personal control? It doesn't belong to them. We must take responsibility for our own thoughts and actions, knowing we affect those around us. *We* decide if our energy is positive or negative. The discovery of our purpose can fuel our passion, as well as direct our thoughts and actions, which will guide us to success.

When we choose gratitude, compassion, and positive words and actions, we create more than just our own fulfillment and joy—we spread that to others.

Take a moment today to think about how you present yourself to others. Only you know if that is satisfactory. If it is, then continue to grow and expand in your beautiful manifestation. If not, then take the steps to create the vision you wish to see for yourself. We each have the choice to be the person we wish to be. It begins today.

How exciting is that?

We can know that our mistakes and failures can be steps forward to our success. Mistakes and failures are a part of life that can bring us new direction and wisdom. We can learn and evaluate as we journey on our life's path. Let's be grateful and loving to ourselves whether we fail or succeed. The fact that we are learning and making conscious choices every day is really the success.

Suffering comes in many different aspects. What we make of our suffering dictates our personal journey through life—creating a better world. We are each given different opportunities through life. Our individual power of choice directs how we proceed with the circumstances presented to us. At times, opportunities can be missed due to our not giving these opportunities our attention. We overlook the occasion, often doubting our ability to move forward on the opportunity.

Daily, we can open our eyes to new discoveries, new wisdom, and new experiences— including any failure that can become new opportunity in disguise. Sometimes, it's difficult to see the positive when we feel we have failed. We may struggle to understand what we must do differently in a particular situation. Always, we can choose to use our energy to accept our current situation or just step back and take a look at where we are (with a compassionate view). Using love and compassion to find a new perspective allows us to find and then focus on a new action that will move us forward in a more positive manner. Remembering that the mindset and actions we take set the direction of what we will manifest allows us to choose love and joy as we work through decisions.

Let me again stress that going into any forward movement (mentally or physically) requires an attitude of trust.

This is vital!

With trust, we open the door to the beautiful, positive creation—possibly beyond our goals and dreams. Don't limit yourself to just what you envision. So many unimagined, wonderful things may be waiting for you. Do not fear the unknown situations that lie ahead because, truthfully, every new day is an unknown.

Remember, the mind is exceptionally powerful. Our choices define us. Use these choices to enhance your life. The effect of a focus on solutions, rather than on challenges, changes everything. You can look at the triggers in life to get an idea of where to shift focus to a solution-based intent:

- Surroundings
- The effect others have on our happiness
- Connections made
- Experience and challenges
- Consideration for how something can be faced differently

Don't chase life. Allow life to flow. We cannot undo the past but we can look forward to the future.

> *"What you can do is often simply a matter of what you will do."*
>
> **~Norton Juster, *The Phantom Tollbooth***

HAPPINESS AND POSITIVE OUTLOOK – THE EF-FECT ON OUR PHYSICAL HEALTH

We can prevent negative thoughts by creating and re-placing those with positive thoughts. For example: consider facing each day in an attitude of gratitude and compassion.

Our thoughts move us to our personality. Our thoughts reside in us energetically. When you think: "I am health" or "I am joy" or "I am love," your thoughts move you to your personal reality. Thoughts create the reality we mag-nify around ourselves. How we choose to educate ourselves also creates what resonates within us. The direction of our thoughts guides our energy and what, then, becomes our reality.

So, what is our mind? Our mind is a collection of person-al thoughts and beliefs.

What if our thoughts were always positive and balanced? The *negative* cannot stick to us. Negativity may pass through, but positivity will prevail.

It's a law of truth.

Consider someone you know who constantly views life with a "glass half empty" attitude. That person's negative mindset allows fear and pessimism to consume his or her thoughts. A positive mindset will not allow fear and negativity to control it – there is an energetic wall blocking that adverse attitude from penetrating. Positivity will not allow a negative energy to control it.

How is our health affected by our thoughts? The mind, actually, can be a trigger for wellness or illness because what we think has a direct effect on the cells of the body. Stress and fear trigger an auto-immune response sometimes referred to as a "fight or flight" response. Cortisol is released under perceived stress from the mind and the body reacts—kicking in a physiological response to this powerful hormone.

This is significant because the manner in which we respond to challenges can directly lead to illnesses from overworked, over-stimulated body systems. For example, when faced with a stressful situation, if we relax, think things through, and decide what our response will be with an open and compassionate mindset (looking at various perspectives), we are able to avoid the anxiety and resulting physiological response to fight or run from the situation. It is easy to come to the realization that those actions (calming ourselves, observing, then choosing how to react) are more important than the stressful situation itself!

Stress is definitely out there, but *we choose* how we will be affected. In addition, when we stop to think things through and then decide what our response will be, always keeping an open mind, we can actually minimize the stress and/or anger associated with any situation. These chosen, controlled reactions affect our health every day.

When our mind experiences a thought, it creates a mental picture. Think, for a moment, about the types of pictures you want to create today. The choice is yours!

How exciting is that?

Wow!

CHAPTER 5

"FILTERS"

"Don't change so people will like you. Be yourself and the right people will love the real you."

~Kristin Richardson Jordan

All of the above is great in theory, you might be thinking, but what about the effect of others on us? Do we filter how we are influenced by others?

How do other people bring joy or sadness to us?

When we allow others to irritate us, we succumb to their influence and allow their energy to decide our joy, or lack of it. We can always make a choice—become irritated and let that consume us, or look at others objectively and with a calm, open mind.

Think: "What attitude do I take in this particular situation? What steps do I take?"

This reminds me of my many years working in my restaurant, interacting with the public day-in and day-out. Customers were always found in a variety of moods. Occasionally, I would sense a customer being negative and irritated—almost looking for something to complain about. I chose not to become irritated myself, but instead, to actually see this situation as a challenge. I thought: "*What can I possibly do to lift this person to a more positive, happy mood?*"

After some consideration, I would do my best to make that person feel welcomed. I would strive to give great service, and share a smile. I was always amazed at how many times the energy would shift and the mood of that person lift. It would come as a returned smile, a "thank you" or a compliment.

This filled my heart with joy.

How do we filter or process *those* difficult situations in which we become irritated?

Great question!

Doing for ourselves allows us to share our love—it goes in many directions, which lets us cherish and enjoy the things we love to do, as well as look ahead to new moments. All of this allows us the joy of discovering even more things that we love to do.

We can put so many measures into our happiness. We may think: "I must have this" or "I must accomplish that." These demands cause us to withhold the joy that we have available to us moment by moment by placing a "when-if" wall to our self-satisfaction.

An option that we can choose instead is: "I am grateful for this…" We can also find joy and excitement in the knowledge that positive goals and efforts we make to strive for excellence really just enhances our life overall. It is fascinating to discover how our paths can come to be completely different from what we originally envisioned them to be. It's almost magical, actually.

An example of this happened during my restaurant adventure. I found a way to tap into happiness each moment of work—that spark of gratitude changed my life. It didn't mean that I was without stress or challenges, it meant that I chose to give what made me happy and fulfilled my focus.

So, the question lingers: How do we work on our desires for the days and years ahead if we focus only on the moment?

Here's my take on it—it's a bit like multi-tasking!

Throughout each new day, we have thousands of thoughts that run through our minds. I find this very exciting and inspiring, really. Every new day can be a series of life adventures. These experiences can be savored each moment—they are present moments that build into a mountain of experience.

Adventure can be created in our mind as we think about the future. The thoughts that we give to the moments in life can create special memories. Each of these memories creates joy in the moment.

There is also something I refer to as, "Put the brakes on!" moments. For example, I may be taking a walk and enjoying my surroundings in the moment. Suddenly, I may have the thought to "Put the brakes on!" and just stop—take a look around and fill myself with gratitude for this particular moment in my life. I will then give myself the gift of a few extra minutes to feel and appreciate this special time—a precious adventure that is savored instead of passed through.

Another example might be while babysitting my grandchildren. Usually, these times are very busy, hectic, and fun. I might, once again, "Put the brakes on!"—choose to just cherish and be thankful for this adventure in my life.

There are multiple moments in life in which we can stop and take time to realize how wonderful life can be. It's so easy to rush through these precious, fleeting moments in our busy lives, then later realize we have missed them—valuable nuggets of time that are gifts to bring us joy. Taking a few moments with a loved one, a beloved pet, a friend, doing something you love, or a remembrance of a personal experience can truly raise the bar on our happiness scale. At any time of the day, we can stop and ask ourselves "Where am I on my happiness scale?"

Choice is such an important factor, that this quote bears repeating:

> *"Attitude is a choice. Happiness is a choice. Giving is a choice. Optimism is a choice. Kindness is a choice. Whatever choice you make, makes you. Choose wisely."*
>
> **~ Roy T. Bennet**

INTENTION

What about intention?

This is a concept that is sometimes difficult to understand completely. I touched on manifesting through intention earlier in this book. Let's explore intention a little more.

Belief and trust are paramount to manifesting—they are the glue that makes intention stick. When you say your intention, if you do not believe and trust you will receive, you are only speaking the words. Even tho, words do have vibration, when you speak with trust, you send magnified positive energy. Doing so, with trust, sends a message to Source and raises you to a higher energy frequency. It is not possible to rise to a higher vibrational consciousness if you refuse to release the lower frequency of doubt or fear.

First, you must recognize yourself as a being of frequencies. Practical requirements found in everyday life, at home, and with others, etc. is frequency vibration. Energetic spiritual requirements of life raise our vibration to the level of our soul's purpose, which then becomes clearer to us.

Remember angels and Source are always supportive of us. Creating the flow of higher vibrational energy captures the inspiration of your soul, which consciously chose this life at this time.

Don't be in judgment of yourself. Instead, feel good that you critique your thoughts and actions as you manifest a more positive and fulfilling life path.

Be open to experience and enjoy the happiness in this lifetime. Be at peace. Honor who you are. You are awesome.

CHAPTER 6

"SUFFERING"

This is such a painful experience—something that presents itself in many different ways to each of us. Our experience with suffering is personal and unique. What we make of that suffering is our personal test. We are in charge of the steps we take through our personal struggle. We are the captain of our own journey.

But what if we regret choices we have made in the past?

Everyone has regrets. The test is still how we handle challenges—even the challenge of regret. Choice can be so difficult to make, especially when we are stressed and emotional.

So, what if we just don't know how to proceed?

Remember, we have access to tools and steps that we can take.

First, just take some long, deep breaths—look at the situation. Perhaps make a list of the possible reactions to the dilemma.

Next, think about what each option, each possible choice that you make, what it could manifest. Consider what a particular remedy could trigger. Keep in mind that a step in any direction begins a new path in life.

Then, sit back and look at each option with an attitude of love and compassion. Ask yourself: "How will this step affect the future?" What effect am I striving for? Are there multiple combinations of steps that could manifest great energy? Are there risky options or choices that could generate negative energy? Additional consideration would include thinking about how a particular move would affect others. How will your decision affect the environment?

After calmly looking at options, make the choice of steps forward that you wish to take. These thoughts and steps will move you forward on your life's path. Taking you in the direction that you have chosen.

Does this take courage?

Absolutely! Many times, with love and trust, we find strength and courage to make a choice that brings about a positive manifestation. In all of this, love and caring is our greatest strength.

Excitement or anticipation can trigger courage within. Even though we may have doubt or fear nipping at our heels, the excitement for what we will see happen in our life enables us to walk through mud to get to the sand.

VIBRATION AND FREQUENCY

So, how do we approach a problem or challenge in life?

We remember our choices: We can move into fear, anger or other low vibrational energies that take power away...or we can align ourselves to the higher frequency emotions of love, compassion and trust that will indeed empower us.

Choosing the higher frequencies creates a magnificent opening into the power of Source and opens the door to amazing, powerful manifestation. Remember, when we choose joy and light, we transform our vibrational energies to a higher enlightened level. When our thoughts and intentions are trust and love (not fear and ego), everything in our path changes.

We also manifest healthy emotions. Our entire energy field allows us to be a creator when we choose to believe and live in love. This gives us confidence as well. Don't choose to be a victim—be a creator!

In choosing this way, we decide between affirmative action or fear-based action. This choice sets the direction of our manifestation. We must be willing to align to a higher vibration. This means to *not* act on fear, ego, or the need for the approval of others. Believe and trust in your alignment—these are daily choices. We can say affirmations, meditate, do everything we are told to do but if there is doubt and a lack of trust, our vibration does not rise to the level possible if we believed and envisioned our affirmations already achieved in our lives. You can ask yourself "How will this manifestation feel?" It shall feel Wonderful!

You may also ask, "So, what do we do?"

We choose love.

Love is a frequency. Love begins with each of us—loving ourselves—and knowing that we are loved by Source, and also loving life around us. In actuality, we are connected to the love of Source. When we align to the higher frequencies of love, compassion, and trust, we vibrate that frequency.

The more that we practice this alignment to a higher frequency, the more effortless doing so becomes.

Love from Source is unconditional. It is not just an attitude—love is aligning with and operating in a frequency.

Be the wave.

Feel the energy of others. Monitor your energy frequencies. A lower frequency will feel draining. A higher frequency will raise you higher than you realize. Sometimes, even though we may not wish for a change in our life, raising our frequency does so anyway—to a better set of circumstances, for our best interest. This is the time that acceptance of what we cannot change requires that we release it. We simply let go. Then, we can work on what we can control and manifest. Doing so empowers us and raises our frequency.

When it feels as if things are crumbling around us, the crumbled parts of our experience become seeds that blossom into a new life path.

Can others truly affect our choices?

Absolutely! So, what direction should we take to plan our desires?

Many outside forces can affect the direction we take. We may have people in our life who give us comfort and new perspectives. We have the opportunity to educate ourselves. We meet, read about, or listen to the stories of inspirational people. This can affect us in a tremendous way.

It can mean so much to know we aren't alone—to understand the suffering of others. We can build on the ideas and these experiences of others. We can move beyond suffering through experiencing stories, gleaning from another's wisdom, and learning of someone else's accomplishments.

I am always touched by the heartwarming stories of those who have endured horrific suffering and challenge, particularly when they have taken a path to help others as a result of their experience. Finding joy and fulfillment in the compassionate direction of their lives, these people are "angels on earth"—messengers, as I often refer to them.

During a time of suffering, we all struggle to imagine happiness. These times are times of change, and with all change, new doors will open. We may (even now) have a different life than first imagined. We can have a good life.

The path through our life's journey is discovered one day at a time—one moment at a time. We don't have to accomplish success, joy, or all of our desires at once. We can take steps and relish the moments as we experience them, even slowly. We can also change direction at any time.

How do we affect the suffering of others?

Every single day, our words and actions affect and influence others, whether we realize it or not. Just by what we say or the subtle things we do, we can bring joy—benefitting others—to people, animals, our planet. We have the opportunity to have compassion and caring. It may be as simple as a hug or a smile, inspiration, education, a donation of time and energy to help others.

What we say and do can greatly ease someone else's suffering.

When we realize the vast amount of suffering around us, we have two choices: we can block it out, ignore it, or we can acknowledge it with compassion and caring. In this, we connect with others and give of ourselves—an opportunity to make a difference.

Wanting others to be happy can be a great challenge or struggle for many of us. As an individual, we see so many people and sense the unhappiness in some. This can trigger sadness and a wanting in us because, deep down, we wish to see people filled with joy and gratitude.

We must also remember that every individual is the creator of his or her own thoughts. Others also manifest for themselves. That said, we can still be a positive, outside influence on people because our energy is also felt by others.

CHAPTER 7

"ENERGY"

Did you know that your energy can be felt by others over the telephone? It's true! Energy can be felt by people in a completely separate location, like a neighboring room. You can share your energy (knowingly or unknowingly) via a photograph!

We all resonate on a low-to-high vibration scale. We all have ups and downs. Others feel the energy that we share in so many ways. Consider your words. Words contain not just a message, words convey a feeling and an intention. The words we choose to say give others a sense of what we are feeling. Also, if we are making a particular statement but not feeling the truth or intention of what is spoken, others will feel that in the energy attached to those words. If we don't trust or believe in what we are saying, it shows itself in our vibration. Doubt or disbelief will lower the vibration that *we* feel, as well as what *others* feel from us.

The tone of our voice gives off energy as well. If we are speaking in a calm, compassionate voice, others feel that caring and compassion. The same is true for an angry or critical voice that will send a negative energy to those who hear us. As you go through your day, do you ever take a moment to listen to the tone of your voice? That can be quite eye opening.

The realization of the powerful effect of our vibration and energy on ourselves, as well as others, can be life changing. When we focus on the energy we create in our daily life, taking charge of that energy and creating positive mindset and actions, we will see increased health, success, and abundance in our lives—and, of course, increased happiness. With this, we will also be a tool for others to find this happiness as well.

Powerful stuff, this energy we all have…isn't it?

THE EFFECT OF OTHERS ON OUR LIVES

"The only person you should try to be better than is the person you were yesterday."

~Matty Mullins

We benefit from others' positive energy the same way they do from ours. Through our compassion and caring, others can feel good and be drawn to positive thoughts or feelings

Do other people really control our happiness? The answer is: Only if we allow it. It's as simple as that.

When I look back to the time of my high school years, I remember an incident that impacted me for the rest of my life. This single event changed my perspective about myself and others completely.

Let me tell you what happened…

I had gone out on a couple of dates with a very nice young man and was hoping he would ask me out again. It was around this time that I was asked out by a "very popular" young man in our school to go to a drive-in movie with him. I was never one of those so-called "popular girls," so I was a bit surprised he even knew who I was, let alone ask me out to a movie.

I mentioned what had happened to a few friends but also shared with them my confusion because I didn't really know him and really didn't have any interest in him at that time. In fact, I confided that I really had a crush on the school mate that I had recently began dating.

These friends convinced me that I was crazy for liking the school mate instead of the "popular boy", and that I absolutely could not pass up the date with this "popular guy". It was obvious my friends were excited for me.

I decided to follow their advice and responded that I would go to the drive-in movie with him. Near that same time, the boy whom I had a crush on asked me what I was doing for the weekend. I told him my plans. Nothing more was said.

Saturday arrived and my date picked me up and off we drove to the local drive-in movie theater. We parked, picked up some snacks and settled back in his car to watch the movie together.

About halfway through the movie, he started making sexual advances. I had always been a bit naive and really didn't expect his sexual advances. I tried to explain that I wasn't interested, which made him furious. After several more attempts by him, I asked him to take me home. He started his car and peeled out of the drive-in parking lot. Then, speeding up the hill to the street where I lived, then dropped me off at my home without saying a word.

I was shocked and confused. I couldn't believe that his only motive in asking me out was to get me in the back seat of his car. He wasn't interested in knowing me as a person at all. After that, to my dismay, the young man, who I had been interested in, never asked me out again. I was devastated.

That scenario gave me much to think about – I had a lot to process, but it allowed me to reach a perspective in my life about character and human behavior. I vowed to never judge others by their outside appearance, but rather, to look at the "inside" of a person – find out who that person really is. That promise has stayed with me my entire life.

I believe, we don't know the reason others behave as they do. We just make a decision as to with whom we spend our time and to whom we make commitments. In actuality, I am grateful to the "popular" guy for giving me a life lesson resulting in an eye-opening vision for my life. He, of course, never spoke to me again. But I was totally okay with that. The experience with him taught me to also listen to my inner self. I cannot judge him as to why he treated me that way. I don't know what influences he's had in his life. His decisions are his alone, as mine are mine.

We can always seek advice and assistance from others, but our thoughts and actions will always be of our own creation. At times, when we face criticism or emotional challenges, we can suffer what I call "emotional paralysis". This can stop us in our tracks.

It was around this time in my life that I came up with the phrase: "Love me or not". Of course, I want others to like, approve and love me, but whether people do or not isn't something I can control.

And that's okay!

I strive every day to be the best "me" I can be – the best "me" in my eyes. I also take time to realize my own uniqueness, even though I am far from perfect. Each of us carries our own beautiful uniqueness – something to embrace and celebrate.

Let me share another experience – one that warmed my heart beyond words. The effect of this single event has left a lasting impression that I will never forget. It showed me that there are many among us who will offer kindness beyond our expectation.

I had managed the Tacoma restaurant for many years. I loved my customers, co-workers, and my job in general. The owner had promised me that when he retired, he would allow me to purchase the restaurant. He instructed me to give him a down payment of a mutually agreed upon amount of money. Even though I was a single mother then, I had managed to save and put together exactly the amount I needed to make the down payment on the restaurant. I was very excited about my future in the restaurant. It had been my focus for the future. My personal investment.

One morning, I walked into the restaurant and found him sitting deep in discussion with a couple of gentlemen. I was told that these men were also interested in buying the restaurant. He informed me that if I were to make the purchase, I would need to increase the down payment to $100,000.

I was shocked and dismayed. I proceeded to go to a bank and ask for a loan but was informed that my credit rating wasn't established enough to secure a loan for that amount (I had never really used credit cards in the past). My habit was to pay cash or check for my bills and my record of payment was solid with my mortgage company. That was my history, and it was a good one, but it wasn't enough for a loan apparently.

After being turned down by the bank's loan department, I broke down and cried. My dream was dashed. So many years of hard work and saving seemed lost. I put a question to Source: "Is this truly not meant to be? What is my path then? From here, where do I go?"

After that, I tried to pull myself together and move on. It was difficult because this came on the heels of watching my family go through tremendous sadness. My husband had loved life, loved his family and his job. He had unexpectedly become ill, had multiple surgeries, and then sadly passed away at the young age of 39. What kept me strong during those difficult years was knowing that I had to be there for my children. With the devastation of losing my opportunity to buy the restaurant, my heart wasn't in it anymore.

Later that week, I was chatting with a couple – regular customers of mine. The husband asked me about my purchase plans for the restaurant. I told him that it appeared it wouldn't happen. He pressed me a little and asked why. I explained, as best I could, the situation to which he responded, "Be strong, Paula."

A few days later, to my surprise, there was a knock at the back door of the restaurant. We were preparing to open for the day and didn't expect anyone at that particular time. When the door was opened, a man stood there, explaining he was the accountant for that particular customer. He asked to speak to me.

When I met with him, he retrieved paperwork from a binder – documentation for a loan in the total amount of $100, 000! He said his client, the man I had been speaking with just a few days earlier, wanted to co-sign a loan for me to purchase the restaurant.

I was speechless.

These dear customers had enough faith in me to do this beautiful act of kindness on my behalf. My heart will never forget that moment.

After that, my purchase of the restaurant went through and a year later, I was able to get a loan in my name, solely. I am forever grateful to my beloved customers and friends. We used to have fun joking that I should name a booth after them – not a bad idea, in my mind.

I learned from this that we never really know what may unfold in our life's path. The manifestation that may arise from those around us is real. Whether it be a person or an opportunity, life is full of beautiful surprises.

> *"People take different roads seeking fulfilment and happiness. Just because they're not on your road does not mean they are lost."*
>
> **~Dalai Lama**

I have always loved that thought. Just because people don't share your same path in life does not mean they are lost. It gives meaning to "when our paths cross…" Whenever I meet someone new or reconnect with someone I haven't connected with in a while, I think of this (and say to myself): "I am so grateful that our roads have crossed!"

We don't need to be better than others, we are our own unique beautiful being. When we strive to better ourselves, striving to grow and manifest every day, it is something we do for ourselves – not for others. Those around us feel the effects of who we are and what we strive for.

Don't be afraid to admit to mistakes. Be grateful for criticism. Be open-minded to others' opinions without feeling defensive if you disagree with one another. Choose to stay open to new ideas and filter criticism with an objectivity that resonates truth. Subtle helpful thoughts seep through criticism, if we just learn to filter without defense and keep an open mind about what we are hearing.

When we do these things, we move ahead in our personal path for growth and expand our ability to manifest. Feel the love around you. Let it lift you up. There is more love and support for us than we may actually realize. Take a look around – love comes from many different directions.

CHAPTER 8

"DESTINY"

"When the power of love overcomes the love of power, the world will know peace."

~ Jimi Hendrix

I've often heard the comment, "Life isn't always fair. Get used to it and move on." It's a hard truth that we share with others – a fact of life. What do we gain from this, you may ask? Perhaps just knowing we are not alone in our struggles and suffering, our challenges in life, can relieve the feeling of burden a little bit. Often times, when we are faced with decision, we look to and copy the lives and actions of others – sometimes forgetting that this life is *ours*. We make the choice of where our thoughts and actions are directed. The surroundings we see and the experiences we share bless us with messages and perspectives.

Until we take ownership of our life's path, we don't truly own it. With this realization, we may step up and control our destiny. These are the times in which we calmly, compassionately evaluate what is happening to us and then choose to make positive, loving decisions about the next steps to take.

Doing this can be very difficult, sometimes, particularly when we realize that there are people who could be harming our lives. The understanding that some people actually stop our progression by their actions is painful. People can do things in their own lives that do not enhance ours. When this happens, it takes great courage to say, "I let go of the negative energy you send my way. I let go of my anger and move on in my life."

This is crucial to finding joy and happiness because, remember, anger is an anchor that holds back positive manifestation and happiness. With love and gratitude being our ultimate power, we move on knowing we will create joy and success in our future. In life's journey, we become the perpetual student, always learning, growing and finding new ways to enrich our own life.

Health, love, abundance, and security are common goals . These are goals that we can reach. We can also find happiness in giving ourselves love and gratitude as we take steps every day to move toward our life's enrichment.

So, what can we do to trigger our thoughts and emotions this way?

As mentioned before, trust is a large component. When you have trust, decisions are much easier to make. Also, if we can look at a situation with honesty, we become free from doubt as we make our decision.

Another important aspect is to realize that people (or things) aren't always what they appear to be. When we sit back and take a good look at any situation, always keeping our hearts and minds open to new possibilities, we will see the path that we truly want to follow. As we continue to be grateful for what is positive in life, we find contentment becomes a very strong companion – a force within, as well.

GRATITUDE

"Gratitude is the single most important ingredient to living a successful and fulfilled life."

~Jack Canfield

We can find a way to be grateful in the smallest things. Think about the groceries in your fridge. To have the ability to go to a grocery store and stock a refrigerator with food we find there is something for which to be extremely grateful. When I was a young adult, I realized something that has always guided me to stay focus on gratitude and Joy. I remind myself that I can be just as happy in a cabin in the woods as in a mansion on a hill. I told myself, "My happiness is inside me, not in possessions." Yes, we can find joy and excitement in possessions and monetary achievements, which can be great. But, we actually have access to happiness in our core being. Those extras are just outside triggers. Also, we must guard ourselves that we don't put so much value on the extras, that we create sadness from not having "The things and/or possessions" we believe will make us happy. Deep appreciation for what we do possess and excitement for what we are working to achieve will create contentment and happiness in our being.

In my lifetime, I have travelled to other countries where I witnessed adults and children alike who could not be sure of their next meal. There were people who did not even know where their next drink of water would come from. To be honest, there is hunger in civilizations all around the world. What examples come to you at this moment? Can you name one thing that you are grateful for that is taken for granted by many of us? It's so common to focus only on our big desires and goals, and kind of forget the basic (but *huge*) blessings we already have.

Having the basics, such as food, a bed, and a roof over our heads, is something we take for granted – blessings for which we should be grateful every day of our lives. Think of one thing that you are grateful for every morning. This will start your day with the energy of gratitude. This will be a huge contribution to our goal of increased happiness in our life.

Ask yourself: "What percentage of my day is focused on the positive, rather than the negative?" Live in the moment. Think about how important it is to acknowledge the past.

Though you may occasionally draw upon your memories and experience for inspiration, never idolize the past at the risk of creating a backward drift. The effort should be always to focus on moving forward – to advance.

Choose to be grateful. Doing this one simple thing will absolutely change your life.

When we make the choice to be grateful, it does more than just bring us inner peace and happiness – it gives us strength. Strength carries us through our challenges. We gain wisdom in our times of personal challenge and despair. Be grateful for the new perspectives given through wisdom gained. Often, when we look at situations with new eyes and different perspectives, great creation and energy can arise. Be grateful to those who support us. Take a moment to appreciate and thank them. I believe, we meet those whom we are meant to meet. When you look at life's experiences and relationships in that way, you can ask the question, "What was this relationship or chance meeting meant to teach me?"

When we do this, our vision, emotion, and personal action forward may change. With each new day, we carry new wisdom into the thoughts and actions we give to ourselves and others. To be grateful for those who have affected our lives and helped us choose positive steps forward is another huge contribution to our goal of increased happiness in life.

THE MIND

The mind is exceptionally powerful. Our mind directs our choices. Our choices then define us. We make an active choice to accept our life or to enhance it.

Life is like a river—always moving. At times, we may wish to press the brakes and dwell in a moment, perhaps a beautiful one that we want to hold onto forever, but we are denied. However, with that beautiful moments, we are soon gifted a *forever memory* that belongs to us, to hold, to relish, to keep as ours always.

In our journey called "Life" we have the opportunity to collect many of these special memories. Some may be just simple everyday activities, a routine, a schedule, or something we may consider mundane. However, looking back, once we have moved past that particular phase of life, we may, without realizing it, notice that everyday activity no longer occurs in our life. In fact, we may reminisce about "the time when…" and hold on to those events as precious. Many of those experiences can become life-changing.

I like to refer to what I call, "our mind's library". This is the place in our memory where we may, at any time, pick a moment to reflect upon. This is the place in our minds that our special moments are never lost. They are waiting for us to tap into them—we just need to grasp that moment and experience it again.

Knowing that we are continually moving forward with our collection of moments can bring us joy and a grateful heart. Opportunities for new experiences are ahead. Each new day presents a chance for us to dive into new experience, creativity, and possibility. For example, we can witness a beautiful sunrise, celebrate a new idea, or share acts of kindness with another person or an animal.

When we think about opportunity, we may limit our thoughts to all-encompassing, tremendous achievements. This is great! Living your dreams is remarkable. Still, we don't want to overlook the small joys in life. Publicly unrecognized creation and personal joy may seem small, but these are the stepping stones that take us to greater accomplishments.

Here's to a day of endless opportunity!

Enjoy your moments. Have fun with life. Open your eyes to discover, see new people, gain wisdom.

Even though we may not always see it, failure can actually be opportunity in disguise. Experiencing failure can teach us to become creative and search for new opportunities, to find strengths we may not realize we possess, thus taking us along the road to a very positive outcome.

Life is a process—a continual state of moving. We make constant choices in our reactions to circumstances. Our thoughts become action, particularly when we realize that this is the process of life. We *can* find peace and calm as we work through life's plan for us.

CHAPTER 9

"FOCUS"

"You decide what is important to you by what you dedicate your time to."

~Unknown

Every day, as we choose our thoughts and actions, we are feeding energy. Whether it be positive or negative, we are donating our time and actions to that which we focus on—manifesting as we go along. If we are giving the universe negativity, doubt and anger, we are asking for more of that to be directed back to us in life.

Source listens to what we send out.

If we are directing our thoughts and actions to positivity, compassion and manifestation of that which we desire, we will attract more of the same.

When I struggle with a challenge or find myself in a difficult situation, I ask myself, "Do you want more of this pain and the anxiety that goes along with it? Wouldn't you rather create change and bring in positive energy for empowerment?"

The answer is obvious…YES!

I have to remind myself that even though I may not understand what may come through to put me on a positive path, I know and trust that all things are possible—even the really great stuff! I only need to trust and allow it to happen.

Disruptions happen. Events can arise that pull our attention away from joy. Such distractions as irritation (think: traffic and drivers that cause irritating situations), frustration, discouragement. We constantly see examples of road-rage that can create all three emotional responses in the same moment!

One day, I was driving to pick up my granddaughter from the bus stop. She was returning home from school and I was excited to see her. I had left home, allowing extra time for traffic slow-downs. Normally, I reach at the bus stop early and relax for a few moments while waiting for her to bus to arrive. On this particular day, I ran into stopped traffic. No one was moving anywhere and I was stuck in the middle of this traffic jam, waiting for something to shift. Still, no one moved. The minutes began to tick by and my stress level rose. There was no way around the stopped traffic and no way to get to my granddaughter.

Finally, the traffic began to inch forward. By that time, I was so stressed over the thought of my granddaughter hopping off the bus with no one to greet her that I could barely think. When I finally was able to resume my trip, I sped up and drove much fast than I normally drive. I passed other drivers, realizing I was irritating them as I went by. I began to think about how these drivers had no way of knowing the amount of pressure I felt.

That experience helped me to realize that, at times, I have become irritated with other drivers without knowing exactly what they were experiencing at that time in their lives. From this, I broadened my perspective and now try to think about why someone may seem critical or rude.

I realized that I cannot let others steal my happiness. Joy is mine to own—it belongs to me, not anyone else.

From that day forward, I have more compassion for others, realizing that I cannot know their inner challenges or circumstances. This experience in the car that day gave me a greater sense of peace in my life...in spite of the stress.

In any work environment, we can focus on our tasks and abilities and feel good about who we are, knowing that we are of value. This can bring a joy to us in knowing our personal commitment to work or our creative passion.

Others feel the fulfillment that radiates from us as we make positive efforts to succeed in our mission or task. That, in itself, may affect the energy of those around us in a positive way. Just as we choose the direction of our thoughts and actions, we choose which emotional trigger we give our attention to. Is our intention to enjoy the moment we are in—to be excited for what may manifest in life...or is our intention to look for that which angers us—things that we want but don't have? Anger and resentment creates more anger and resentment in life. Trust and gratitude, actually, creates more to be grateful for.

Live in the moment. It is important to acknowledge the past and, though you may occasionally draw upon your memories and experiences for inspiration, never idolize it at the risk of creating a backward drift in spite of all efforts to advance.

YOU ALONE CONTROL YOUR HAPPINESS

There is reason for good cheer. What you can be and what you can do is largely determined by the attitude you hold most of the time. Attitude is a state of mind that grows until it circles itself with images of its own likeness.

Your attitude reflects how you look at life, whether you see it as vibrant, exciting, busy, full of vivid impressions and new experiences, or whether it needs shining with a positive mental attitude.

Happiness comes from within the self. It is self-starting, self-perpetuating, and self-rewarding. It is in our hearts waiting to be discovered, and you are the explorer!

The sign of true success is a happy heart! Celebrate the gift of life! Find joy in your accomplishments. Be grateful for all you have accomplished and all that you will accomplish. Gratitude is a beautiful, joyous gift. When we love and appreciate ourselves and others for the beautiful individuals we are, we become a beacon of love and inspiration, lighting the way for others.

How Fantastic!

Reaching out with love and gratitude can lift our spirits. We can make the choice to be grateful, love more deeply, and show compassion to those still in our lives.

Personally, I feel crushed when I witness cruelty and death occurring to animals and people. It's like I'm frozen in sorrow. But then, I realize that my anger and sorrow actually give me courage and strength. I become determined to do more to help others, to show kindness to animals.

I choose to make a difference.

For example, we can we can be a positive force against animal cruelty by speaking out, signing petitions, donating time and money to animal causes. There is a big difference between expressing horror at a situation or crying out, "Shame on them!" Or actually doing something about it. Actively protesting the situation by doing something actively to help make the situation better is a choice. Love and compassion are the most powerful of emotions, and creators of strength and perseverance.

When we focus our thoughts and behavior into positive, life-changing acts, we achieve a greater sense of fulfillment and happiness within ourselves.

TOOLS FOR INCREASED HAPPINESS

No one can stop me!

It's true. When I choose to be happy, literally, *no one* can stop me from feeling happiness. I have lived by this belief for most of my life. Admittedly, at times I struggled. It would take all my strength to admit to myself, "Yes! I do have challenges and sadness from heartbreak, but I can still choose joy!"

I will never forget the day that I was informed that one of my brothers had passed away. This was unexpected and happened only a few days before Christmas. Needless to say, that time of year is one of the busiest and for me, it was no exception, particularly at my restaurant. We had one day left to remain open for business before closing for the holiday break. I went to work, knowing my employees and customers needed me there. Behind the tears, I smiled. To say this was one of the most difficult times of my life is an understatement. But I knew I had to make a choice.

Only two days earlier, I had spent the entire day with my brother. Talking and enjoying our time together. The tears began to well again as I thought of our recent time just a couple of days ago. Suddenly, I remembered all the times he had helped me with repairs on my car and with the restaurant. He was a carpenter by trade and always found projects and the time to support me. Remembering his love and caring compassion for me, his sister, brought back a new joy and gave me the strength to go forward that day.

I will forever be grateful to him for what he meant to me, as well as how he impacted my life.

When we lose someone dear to us, often, our first reaction is anger. I know it was for me. A different perspective followed with the arrival of the memories of love and caring. That, alone, deserves my gratitude. With gratitude comes joy and happiness in the acknowledgement of the person's (my brother's) effect on my life. I experienced this gratitude shift, knowing he is watching me from above. My brother would want me to smile as I think of him—not suffer in sadness or anger.

Again, we choose the direction we want our thoughts to go. Do we choose anger and resentment because a loved one has passed? Or, do we choose happiness and joy because of the gift of having that person in our life?

I chose gratitude and happiness. Without a second thought, I knew I was blessed to be his little sister. To this day, whenever I think of my brother, I smile and my heart is warmed.

> *"Never do things for money. It's always the things you do for love that turn out to pay the best."*
>
> **~ Eric Idle**

This is a powerful statement. When our focus is only on the money, we may actually limit our success. However, when our efforts come from service, caring and helping others, we open the doors and windows to success – even beyond our dreams.

In all my years as a restaurant owner and manager, I wanted the business to succeed financially, of course. Throughout this time, however, my focus remained on service to my customers and care of my employees. This came back to my business tenfold. Our customers were like family. Years later, I still see my restaurant customers. These chance meetings lead to great moments chatting and sharing precious memories.

In my Reiki practice, as well, I have never focused on the money. Clients and students come to me in abundance. I am living evidence that this works!

When our passion is for the good of others, we become aligned with the most amazing manifestation energy. How wonderful is that?

CHAPTER 10

"HABITS"

This word can make us cringe. After all, aren't most habits bad and need to be changed? That depends, we can create good habits, but it can often be easier to stress over the bad ones.

We first make habits and then those habits become us. There are two types of habits we typically transition into daily life:

- Intentional habits
- Unconscious habits

We can strive to create habits that we hope to aid us in our desired achievements. The habits can be so many different things: thoughts, affirmations, facial expressions, food, exercise, words, etc. We set a plan in place to implement positive routines. This actually brings us joy, excitement, and a sense of being in change for our betterment.

As we accomplish improvement, we create a sense of satisfaction in ourselves. What if we fall short of our expectations? Ultimately, it's okay! We can find happiness and contentment in knowing what our intent was and realizing life teaches us to walk one step at a time. Remember, it's not about how fast you accomplish your goals, it's about continuing to progress forward. You can take pride in doing that.

The other habits fall into the category of habits we create unconsciously. Typically, we aren't aware that we are creating these habits.

As defined:

hab·it

/ˈhabət/

noun

a settled or regular tendency or practice, especially one that is hard to give up.

"this can develop into **a bad habit**"

custom, practice, routine, wont, pattern, conven-
tion, way, norm, tradition, matter of course, rule, usage

"it was his habit to go for a run every morning"

mannerism, way, quirk, foible, trick, trait, idiosyncra-
sy,peculiarity, singularity, oddity, eccentricity, feature;-
tendency, propensity, inclination, bent, proclivity, dis-
position, predisposition, "her many irritating habits"

accustomed to, used to, given to, wont to, inclined to

"they were in the habit of phoning each other daily"

Take a few moments and make a list of the behaviors
you believe are your habits (this can actually be quite fun!).
Look at your list. You might chuckle when you observe your
unique behaviors listed on paper. Don't forget to include
your *thought* habits (thought patterns that become habitual).   What habits do you want to phase out? What habits
do you want to continue? Consider the list as a catalyst for
ideas – new habits that you would like to implement.

Let's look more at our thought habits. Oftentimes, we
don't realize how our thoughts have become habitual. In
looking at the list, we can recognize similar reactions occurring with different situations. This is initiated by a thought
pattern, most often. Consider the result: Is it good for you?

Is it detrimental? Look at these reactions from thoughts and make the distinction.

Sometimes, we wish that we weren't different from others. Remember, our unique differences are what make us special. When we are grateful for who we are, and cherish our individual qualities, we not only feel joy, but we are able to grow and manifest more of our own magnificence. We become free when we let go of what others expect from us. Feeling at peace with ourselves more and more often, creates a habit of automatically generating that thought pattern. Thus creating an emotional habit. Eventually, you're feeling good without thinking about it.

When we need to examine what thought habits we are creating, it can be a struggle to examine our thoughts objectively—to see which ones are not supporting the direction we wish to take. This is where the power of decision comes into play. Every decision, or choice, sends that energy into motion. Filtering and directing our thoughts truly is a lifetime process. We draw into our lives what we put out. Take a moment to be aware of what thoughts and reactions come to your mind automatically in most situations.

Which of these are positive and beneficial? Which are not? You may even create a practice of making notes to objectively evaluate your habitual thoughts and reactions.

We can at any time make the decision to focus our thoughts in a different direction. Letting ourselves look at situations or emotions simply with a new perspective can turn the reaction, the energy, and the manifestation in a new direction. Then, as we push ourselves in this shift on a daily basis, it will soon become automatic! Just imagine the shift we can empower ourselves to create in our daily life. It really is fascinating and inspiring.

In my Reiki practice, I feel that experiencing my own physical pain and heart wounds has given me the opportunity to come closer to having a compassionate, understanding of life's challenges. This has indeed changed my thought process. The habit, you could say, that my perception and daily practice has created in my mindset. I pushed myself not to focus on the "Why me?", or the anger and resentment, but instead, to focus on what these challenges have shown me, as well as giving me the appreciation of the blessings and memories that I cherish.

Experiencing your own pain brings greater understanding of others' pain and increased compassion for them. This can be viewed as a gift, a new perspective. Experiences can totally change our thought patterns, consciously or subconsciously. When thought patterns have consistency and repetition, they become an unconscious habit pattern. I see the scope of my thought patterns as a large spinning wheel, with multiple choices, and I choose where it will stop. There are many choices available to us: Joy, Excitement, Love, Inspiration, Abundance, Manifestation, Enlightenment, Anger, Jealousy, Doubt, and resentment. Where do you want to be on your spinning wheel?

Habits can be things around us that we give our attention to everyday.

For example, Angels.

Angels, guides, loved ones who have passed, and others are always with us. Knowing this can be a source of profound joy. It gives us the *knowing* of how much we are loved. Even when we may feel totally alone, we can *know* we are not alone. We know that we are surrounded by love and support at all times.

I, personally, start every day asking the archangels and others to be with me, to love me, to guide me, and to protect me. My thankfulness and expressed love for them is also a daily practice (sometimes minute by minute). This time to express my gratitude and ask for support every day sets the tone for my day. Doing so fills me with gratitude and excitement for what my life's journey has yet to show me. I have no fear because I know I am loved and supported, even with my imperfections.

While on this earth, there are many people who love and support us, as well as a few who challenge or hurt us. In the other realm, we have our loving Angels who are willing to wrap their arms around us, protecting and loving us. Additionally, Source, Angels and our guides will put opportunities and relationships in our path. This may look like a coincidence, but generally, these events that show up at "just the right time" in our lives happen not by accident. People you meet, who have a powerful influence on your life, have a purpose for being there. When we say "yes" to manifestation and open our hearts to alternatives, events and opportunities will come to us—prospects that are beyond our wildest dreams.

Seeds come to us, we plant them, and then watch them grow.

What seeds will you plant today?

THE PERSPECTIVE ON AGING

Think about your age. Do you accept the years you've racked up in this life?

One of the best tools for building happiness is to accept our age. Consider this: what happens when we look or yearn for a different time in life—for a different age? There can be a great deal of excitement in an older age—a great time to look forward to.

If we focus excessively on the future, we rob ourselves the gratitude and joy we could experience at the moment—at the age we are currently. At times, we may even look back to the past, at an earlier time in life, and wish for those years again. The same result happens—we are robbed of the present moment and the joy that accompanies it.

The importance of being satisfied and happy in the moment cannot be overstated. When we appreciate each moment, we are filled with a contentment that becomes the tool to real happiness.

When the reverse happens...what then? What if we struggle with aging?

It's not uncommon to yearn for a younger appearance. We may long for our youthful physical fitness. Not being able to move without dexterity or discomfort is disheartening and can lead to depression, even a lack of self-esteem. Frustration with appearance or ability is real and thoughts such as,

"How can I be happy in this state?" often follow. This is where perspective comes into play.

Do you believe beauty lies inside the soul or solely outside in the physical body? Is our heart our core?

When we realize that our true essence is the love within us, we gain true perspective. We all have love, in and around us. Take a close look at your life. Like most, you will experience moments that you would likely react differently to, given the chance. No matter your age, that outlook doesn't change. Hindsight is a great teacher, indeed.

You will experience moments you are proud of, and moments you wish you had handled differently. Let's look at how this works. Consider the wrinkles and grey hair beginning to make their appearance on your body. Does skin and hair change your past?

No!

The essence of our prior path does not change. Our spirit does not grow old. The physical changes that arise as we age can actually open up opportunities not considered before.

We have the chance to access our thoughts and how we view our circumstances in life. Wisdom and experiences are gained in younger years.

This comes with time, which allows us to transform how we view ourselves and others. These tools of awareness can affect what we value in our current stage of life. New perspective will bring peace—the kind of peace that we have never experienced before.

Aging is a time of joy as this is a beautiful time for shifting.

SHARING

Every single day, we share.

Actions, energy, words...you name it, we share. Although we may not always realize it, how we speak affects others. Our words are not only powerful, but the energy behind our words is shared as powerful. Others feel it. This energy dictates the vibration level that we reside in. This vibration affects our manifestations, thoughts, actions, and words.

We can share with others in so many ways. Acts of kindness, caring, inspiration, financial means, or service are all ways to share positively, affecting positive energy and building the vibration to bring the same back to us. We can give of ourselves to animals, the planet and humanity. Everything we do affects who is affected—particularly us!

But how can that be?

When we give, we also give to ourselves. The joy that we find in our heart when we focus on helping others lifts us up. Compassion is powerful. It truly is medicine for the soul and heart. Remember, also, that Compassion and kindness goes both ways. When someone else gives us the gift of compassion, it warms our heart. We feel gratitude and appreciation for that act…that person. The energy we feel is shared and the vibration for all individuals involved rises.

An emotion shared can create a relationship, excitement, or even sadness. Our mood is felt by those around us.

Let's think about how powerful that concept is.

Our emotions, not only, direct our life but also affects the lives of others. For example, imagine you are in a crowded room. For some reason, you feel drawn to one person in particular. This doesn't hold true for a few of the others standing in the room with you. Why is that?

Energy is the answer. The energy vibration is what you are responding to. We express ourselves and the energy reflects that, which can be triggered by our heart, ego, or emotion. Other people do the same. You sense their energy and are drawn or repelled by it.

Ask one question each day: "What energy am I sharing with the world?"

Remember, energy is triggered by thoughts, words, emotions, and actions. All of these are choices made daily by each of us.

What we do may be the change or a step forward toward the good.

Consider the planet. Mankind is the only species with the power to destroy the earth, as well as protect it. What actions can we take to move our world into positive direction? Even though we are only one person, we can act with intention and compassion. As we've been told, a ripple can become a wave.

Let's become that wave together.

> "Positive people give off a special glow. Let's each be one of those people."
>
> **~Paula Vail**

CHAPTER 11

"JOY"

"Don't sweat the small stuff, Paula."

This advice came to me years ago and has never left. I've learned that there is much more attached to that thought—little "nuggets" that bloom into beautiful concepts to lead me toward a more joyous life.

Let me share another with you: don't allow small irritations to steal your joy. Having a precious moment in life is truly a joyous gift to be given. If we let something, such as the loss of ten minutes at an appointment or someone else's rude behavior, steal our "happy to be alive" feelings, we short-change ourselves.

We must realize that life is filled with ongoing, irritation and stress. It's literally a fact of life. We must accept that life isn't perfect either. Knowing this, we shouldn't hold onto the guilt or frustration in that our lives aren't perfect.

It's okay to not be perfect!

Let's not be angry about what life hands us. Others are not perfect either—again, a fact of life. We are all trying and that should be inspiring. Every day is a new day and we can use that day to become a better version of ourselves. Thinking about what we would like to achieve and what inspires us is a tool we can use to increase our happiness.

Another of life's facts: We cannot undo the past.

It's true—though many of us try very hard to do so.

What we can do is let go of our guilt and regret, and take forward the lessons learned, wisdom gained, and perspectives expanded. Learning from the past is a positive step forward. Those positives create new manifestation and creativity. The flow of our life's journey is continual. Thoughts and actions that we contribute to our life helps to create our future. Trust in that process and know that happiness is within reach. It resides within each of us.

Some of my happiness triggers are music, dance, the weather, scenery, and nature. What are yours?

There is nothing quite like hearing a favorite song. The words resonate inside our hearts and, for those few moments, we are consumed by the words and score of that particular song. I believe music is a feel-good tool. Music can take us out of a lower vibration resonance, lifting us to a happier vibration level.

Dance is a direct result of a positive trigger. Dancing is an expression of physical motion as the music resonates through a person. Another fantastic way to increase joy and elevate moods.

Does weather increase happiness?

Think about how it feels when sunlight kisses your skin or a cool breeze blows through your hair on a hot summer day? Nothing compares.

In the middle of a crazy, hectic day, we can step outside and bask in that warm, loving sun energy, shining down upon us. A few relaxing moments in the sunlight can actually give us a reset, especially when accompanied by a few deep breaths. Doing this can relieve stress and give us a recharge during a chaotic day.

Other weather systems can be a source of happiness, as well. Observe the unique and ever-changing clouds. Remember as a child, looking up into the sky and imagining various pictures envisioned in their puffy shapes?

Consider cloudbursts. We can all feel a special kind of tranquility when listening to the rain fall on rooftops. Watching the breeze blow through a tree, lifting its leaves in a dance to enchant us. Witnessing the majesty of a winter snowfall brings peace. Listening to the sound of the waves hitting the shore.

All of these moments with nature's climate can make us happier – precious moments shared with the elements in silence.

Take in the beautiful scenery around you. No matter where you are on the planet, you can find unique beauty around you. We all share the gift of existence on a breathtaking, life-sustaining planet called Earth. Whether you dwell in a forest, live in a desert, stand on top of a mountain, or bask near an ocean, you are given the magnificence, the energy, the wildlife, the gardens…the beautiful environment to relish, wherever you are. Enjoy my friend!

How often do you look at the landscape around you and just take a moment to appreciate and enjoy it? This may be another potential "happiness trigger" for you.

Do you rush up a road, through a trail, or across a field without taking in the view around you? If so, is this because you are focused on where you need to be or what you need to do next? Do thoughts consume you, distracting you from the gift of Mother Earth?

We share a blessing – we dwell on the same earth. This is a gift to us every single day of our lives. The action of taking in and resonating with that beauty, realizing that we are connected to energy and love from Mother Earth, opens our minds and body to the vibration of peaceful earth energy. It can be felt.

This is another trigger that increases joy in everyday life!

Life is full of "happiness triggers." Give yourself more of the things that make you happy. When I hear a favorite song, my mood changes – a very simple but powerful event. I may even sing and dance along to the music. It lifts my mood.

Think about those things that trigger joy in your life? Take a moment to make a list of your "happiness triggers."

What if you chose to give those triggers to yourself every day? When you do, look back at the effect doing so has on your thoughts and emotions of that day.

Each of us can enhance our lives in the simplest ways. Have fun blessing your own life with more "happiness triggers."

CHILDLIKE JOY

Have you ever watched a child at play – exuberant play in which nothing matters but the moment? Do you remember being so joyful that nothing could distract you from the feeling?

Children aren't obsessed with yesterday or tomorrow. As adults, we tend to think only in yesterdays (past) and tomorrows (future). As we age, many of us tend to become more serious about life. We become less in the moment – less into just enjoying the moment, as children do. We become consumed by our responsibilities, money, the influence of others, and so much more.

It is as though we are wearing a heavy jacket that weighs too much for our shoulders to bear. We may tell ourselves,

"I cannot be happy yet. I have too much to do." We might think, "I'll be happy when I accomplish this or that..."

The daily focus on this type of thought pattern actually shuts the door on the small, everyday flow of happiness that we receive from the little things in life.

So, what can we do differently?

We can take time to let go of the "wants" and enjoy the "haves".

CREATING THE PATH

"Do not go where the path may lead, go instead, where there is no path and leave a trail."

~ Ralph Waldo Emerson

Let me share a few steps that I have ingrained into my daily life. Mostly, it's a mental pattern that is set into a routine – this consists of reminders. I remind myself that life is a day-to-day journey and I will strive to do my best. However, I also realize that I will make mistakes, but I will continue on the positive path that I've envisioned for myself. This includes, envisioning where I want to be a year from now.

On difficult days, I stop and picture in my mind exactly what I want to experience in life a year from now. I find joy in my personal version of myself at that time. The vision I have created for the next year allows me to take a moment to glorify my uniqueness, thanking the universe for that moment. Afterward, I sit back and contemplate what I want and why.

I like to ask myself, "Why do I want this outcome?" Doing this requires me to consider my motive and what's behind it. I can then ask, "Is this a motive of good character and compassion? Am I showing respect for myself and others?"

When these questions can be answered in good conscience, I can proceed to work my plan. This begins with realizing the process happens step by step.

In addition, the understanding that I may have to alter the course from time to time is acceptable. I'm okay with that. I vow to accept obstacles that arise, handle those situations with calm, compassion, and reason, and move on.

I begin walking this path and thank myself, feeling good about knowing who I am and that I am moving forward toward my vision. Not every plan is easy. I, too, have discovered several times in life that my path must be altered. There has been sadness and disappointment throughout. This requires incredible flexibility with a keen focus on achieving goals and accepting change.

When our path changes course, it is a new opportunity for us. We may find ourselves on a path that is more exciting and fulfilling than the previous path– something we most likely did not expect. I never dreamed of being a TV and radio host. The opportunity was given to me through a course change, and I have discovered a passion and fulfilment in that job beyond what I had envisioned for myself.

Sometimes we aren't sure how to find our life's purpose or how to reach our full potential. That's okay! We can let life flow and look for signals that guide us to our purpose. We can ask our guides and angels, or whomever we prefer to call upon for direction. They will assist us.

Listen to your heart. Let your intuition speak to you. Celebrate the miracle of that! You are divine and connected to the universe, to Source.

Have fun watching for triggers that will guide and assist you in finding your passion. Spend time doing those things that make you happy. Even if it is a small part of your busy day, pay attention to the signs and details that come your way.

Take the time to allow your happiness to rise and flow through you. Give the beautiful you some time every day to do something you love doing, enjoy something around you, create something that fills your heart, and so on.

Whatever it is that stirs your soul, do it. When we love ourselves, we also have more love to share with others.

FINAL THOUGHTS

Let me conclude with what I believe to be some of the most powerful tools to use to increase happiness:

- Take time every day to be grateful.
- Think about something that you love about yourself.
- Be grateful for someone or something in your life.

Let these thoughts set the tone of your day. Go back to those thoughts at any time you need to remember gratitude. Also, keep your mind and heart open to the beautiful manifestation and joy that comes your way. Let those happy thoughts anchor your heart and body. You will feel the effects, I promise.

Remember, you are the energy you give to Source, reaching into the universe. Holding onto that belief will attract more of what you ask for. *You* are the magic that creates your beautiful and unique life. *You* have the power within you to bring joy, light, love, success, and so much more into your life. I have faith in your abilities. Without a doubt, I know that happiness is yours to enjoy!

I am truly happy for you!

Love…Hugs…and Blessings!

Paula

ACKNOWLEDGEMENTS

The process of writing this book developed from thoughts about all of the individuals who have contributed to my life. These are people who have helped me become the person that I am today. The list is huge!

In this book, I share many of my life experiences and the resulting perspectives I've gained as a result. I am so grateful for the many beautiful life experiences that I have experienced. Even though, not all of my life-experiences has been good. I do want to express my gratitude for their contribution in helping me grow and gain new life perspectives.

During the time my dear "Auntie Jackie" lived, I took advantage of precious time spent with her – laughing and teasing her that "I'm the way I am because of you." We had so much fun together. She and Uncle Ernie were great influences on me. I am forever grateful to them.

It goes without saying that deep appreciation goes to my parents, my children, my pets, and many others. Numerous people have inspired and guided me throughout my life in various ways. To all, I am eternally grateful.

My final expression of gratitude goes out to you, dear reader, for taking the time to consider and choose this book. Reading these pages is the greatest compliment you can give to its author. My sincere wish is that you gain increased happiness, gratitude, and inspiration in your own life.

Thank you so much!

Paula Neva Vail

BIOGRAPHY

Paula Vail is the owner and founder of Wellness Inspired, a television and radio show host, published author, inspirational speaker, actress, and entrepreneur.

Paula's show, *Choices: Finding Your Joy*, is currently broadcast on 1150KKNW, in the Seattle, WA area. Her shows are also broadcast on 5DTV, www.bingenetworks.tv/channel/12673 and YouTube.

She is a featured expert in the upcoming documentary film, *Imagine a World*, scheduled for release in 2019. To find more information go to: https://www.imagineaworldmovie.org/

IMAGINE A WORLD movie. Worldwide Release: Spring 2019.

Paula is a Reiki Master and teacher in the Usui Reiki tradition, Paula has also received training in shamanism and quantum healing practices. Prior to her Reiki practice and radio show, Paula owned and managed a restaurant in Tacoma. For more than 27 years, she worked, finding joy in the service of others in the restaurant industry.

Paula was featured in New York City Times Square by the Continental *Who's Who* organization as a Pinnacle Professional, and has been featured twice in the *Women of Distinction Magazine* for her achievements in business and life. In 2015, she was featured in that year's edition and graced the cover of the 2017 edition. In addition, she has been featured in ICE magazine.

Paula shares the spotlight in the book, *America's Leading Ladies*, which includes other celebrities such as Oprah Winfrey, Melinda Gates, Mary Barra (CEO of General Motors), Virginia Rometty (CEO of IBM), Millika Chopra (daughter of Deepak Chopra), and many other successful, life coaches, Entrepreneurs, CEOs, Radio and TV personalities, and athletes, and more.

Charity work in the US and around the world comprises some of Paula's great loves. You can read more about her charities and information about Paula on her website (see links below).

www.wellnessinspired.com

www.heartsforloveworldwide.org

www.ASPCA.org

www.Orphansafrica.org

Paula's show, *Choices: Finding Your Joy* can be found at:

https://1150kknw.com/www.bingenetworks.tv/channel/

12673 and 5DTV and YouTube.

Contact Paula by email: paula@wellnessinspired.com

CPSIA information can be obtained
at www.ICGtesting.com
Printed in the USA
JSHW022338050919
1378JS00002B/2